Take Away 1 Monkey

3 - 1 = 2

2 - 1 = ____

4 - 1 = ____

5 - 1 = ____

6 - 1 = ____

1 - 1 = ____

one less

4	5		1		6
	2		4		3

How many bananas are left?

5 - 2 = 3

___ - ___ = ___

___ - ___ = ___

___ - ___ = ___

___ - ___ = ___

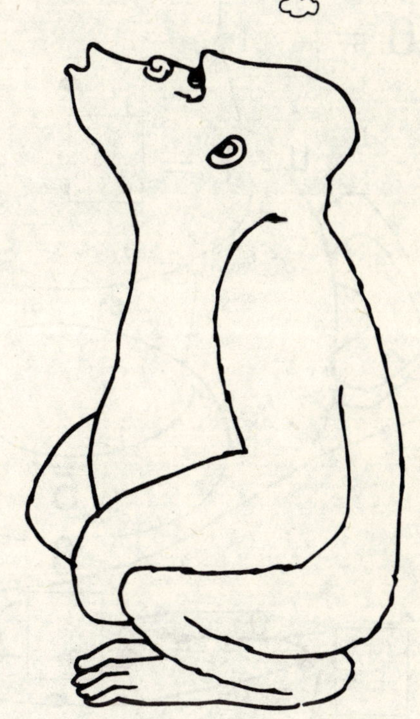

5 - 5 = ______ 5 - 3 = ______

4 - 1 = ______ 4 - 2 = ______

4 - 2 = ______ 2 - 0 = ______

3 - 3 = ______ 3 - 2 = ______

2 - 1 = ______ 5 - 4 = ______

4 - 0 = ______ 3 - 1 = ______

Connect the dots in order.
Start at 0.

Start here.
4 - 4 = 0

4
- 3

4 - 0 =

4
- 2

4 - 1 =

5
- 3

5
-1

Start here.
5 - 5 = 0

5
- 0

5 - 4 =

5
- 2

Can you do these for me?

4 -3 ――― 1	5 -1 ―――	3 -1 ―――
3 -0 ―――	3 -2 ―――	5 -2 ―――
1 -1 ―――	5 - 4 ―――	4 -1 ―――
4 -2 ―――	2 -1 ―――	3 -3 ―――
2 -2 ―――	4 -1 ―――	5 -3 ―――

Match the Monkey

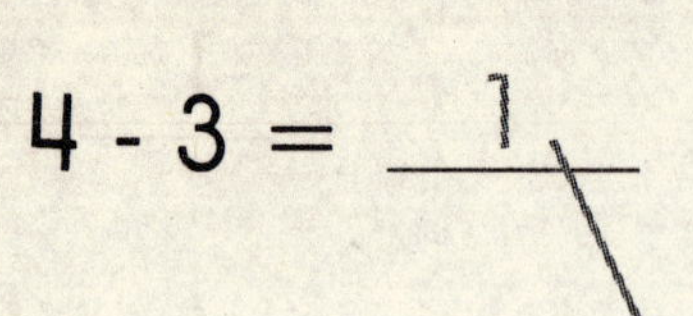

4 - 3 = 1

1 - 1 = ______

2 - 1 = ______

3 - 2 = ______

1

3 - 3 = ______

5 - 4 = ______

5 - 5 = ______

2 - 2 = ______

2

3 - 1 = ______

3 - 0 = ______

4 - 1 = ______

5 - 3 = ______

3

5 - 2 = ______

4 - 2 = ______

How many coconuts are left?

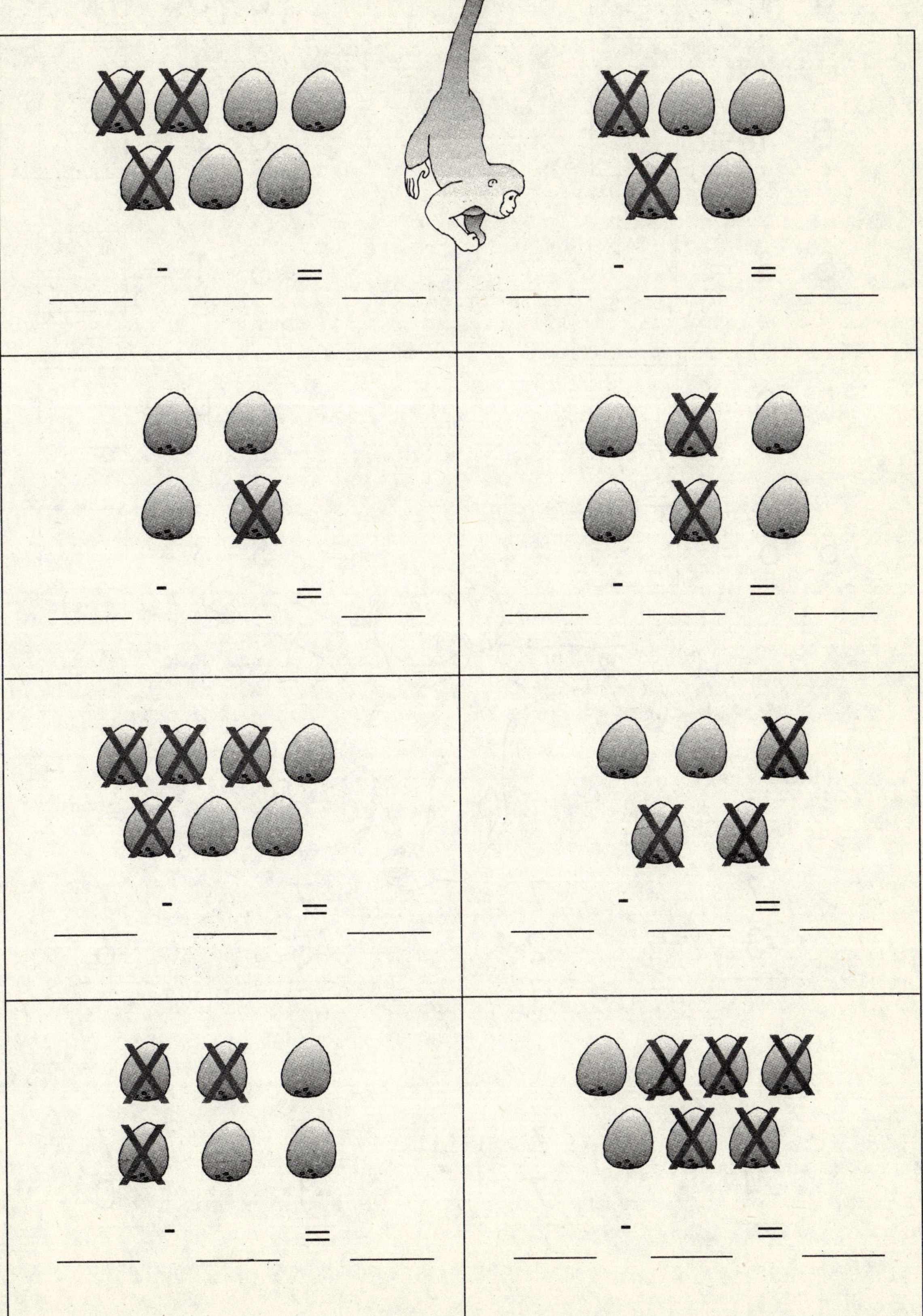

Review

5 - 4 = ☐

5 - 1 = ☐

5 - 3 = ☐

5 - 0 = ☐

5 - 5 = ☐

6 - 5 = ☐

6 - 2 = ☐

6 - 1 = ☐

6 - 4 = ☐

6 - 3 = ☐

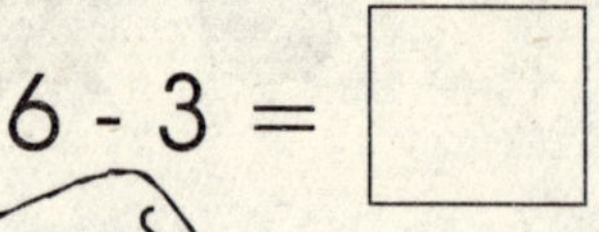

7	7	7	7
-3	-2	-5	-6
___	___	___	___

7	7	7	7
-4	-7	-1	-0
___	___	___	___

How fast can you find the answer?

7	2	4	3	7	5
-4	-0	-2	-3	-1	-2
6	5	5	7	4	2
-2	-3	-5	-5	-3	-1
3	5	7	5	3	4
-1	-4	-2	-1	-2	-4
5	6	4	3	6	5
-0	-6	-2	-2	-0	-0
6	7	6	5	4	6
-5	-6	-4	-3	-3	-1

How many are left?

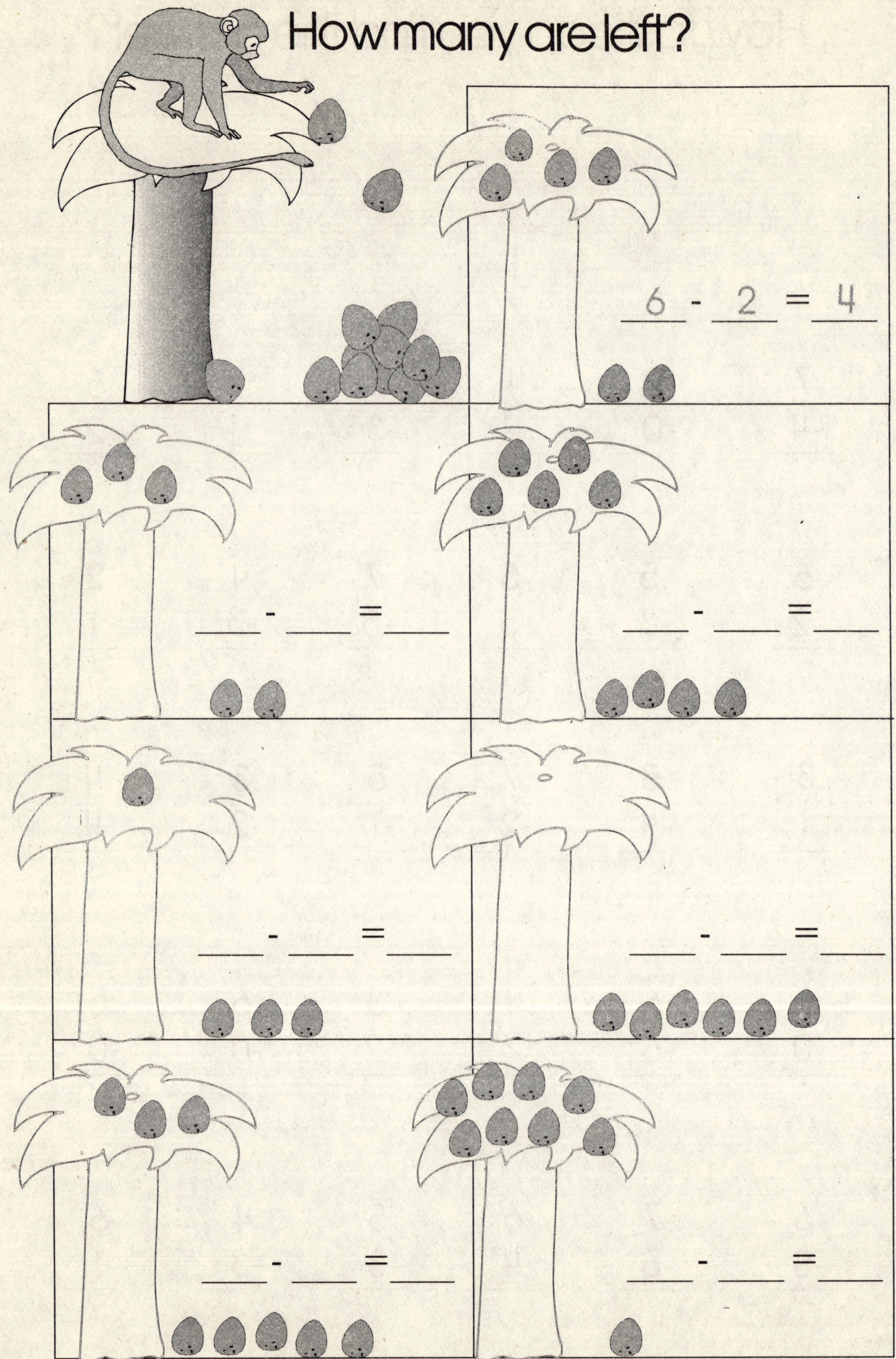

How many did I eat?

8 - 4 = 4

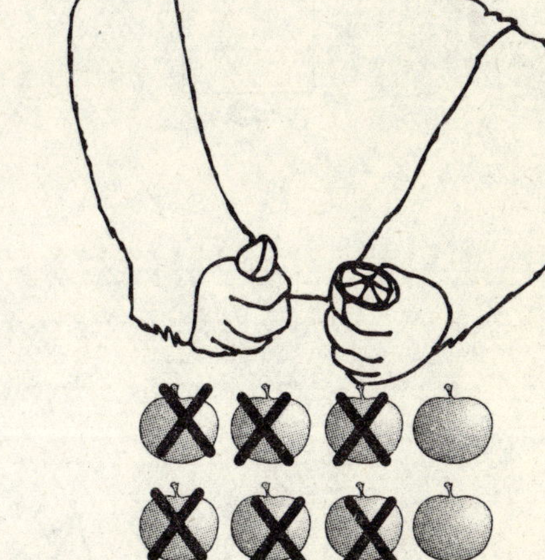

____ - ____ = ____   ____ - ____ = ____

____ - ____ = ____   ____ - ____ = ____

____ - ____ = ____   ____ - ____ = ____

Help the little monkey find her mother.

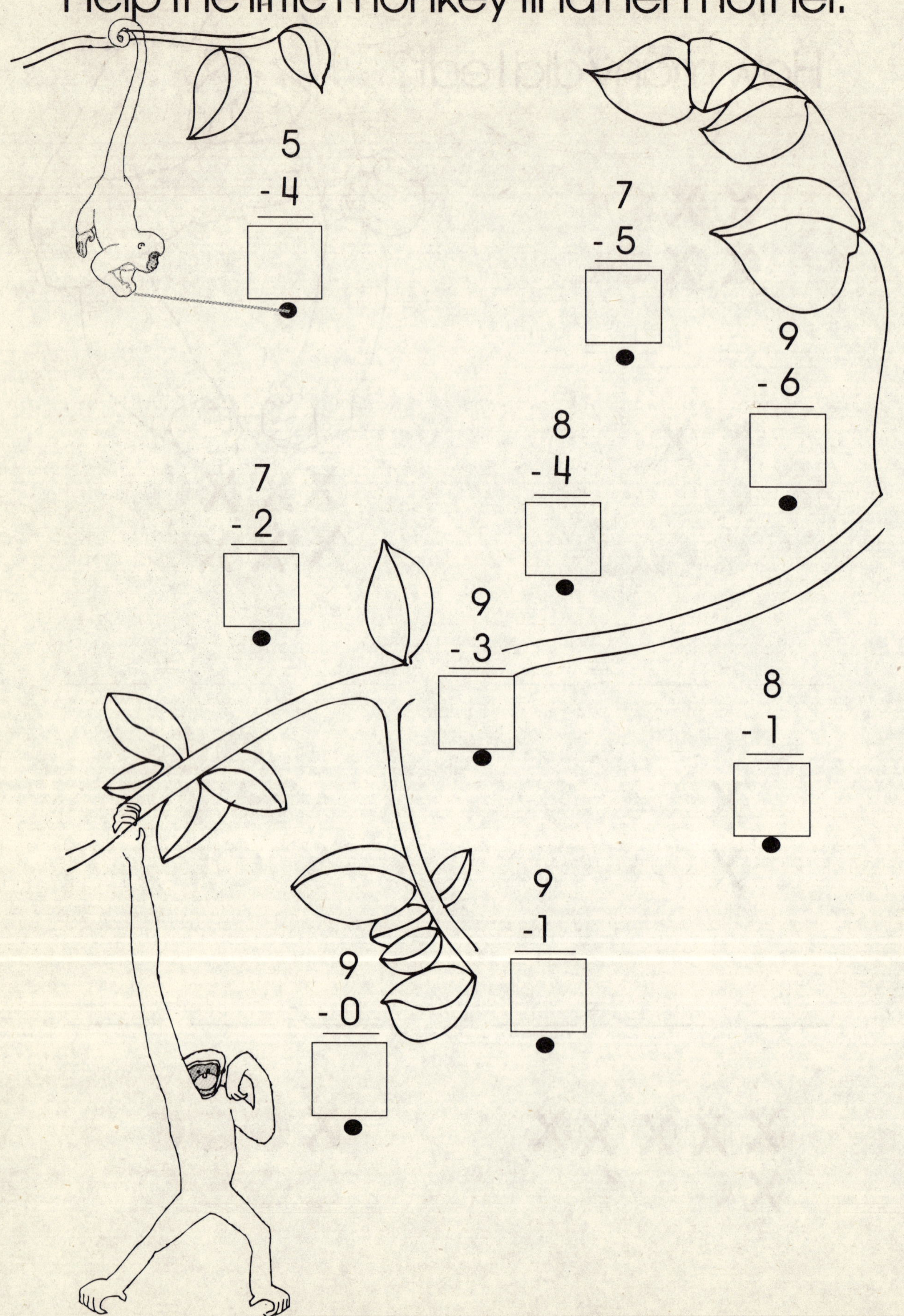

You can find this "key" in the jungle.

8 -3	4 -1	6 -2	9 -3	8 -0	7 -6
		4			
		n			

Draw it here.

1 - y
2 - t
3 - o
4 - n
5 - m
6 - k
7 - j
8 - e
9 - d
10 - a

Show two problems for each picture.

4 - 3 = 1

4 - 1 = 3

____ - ____ = ____

____ - ____ = ____

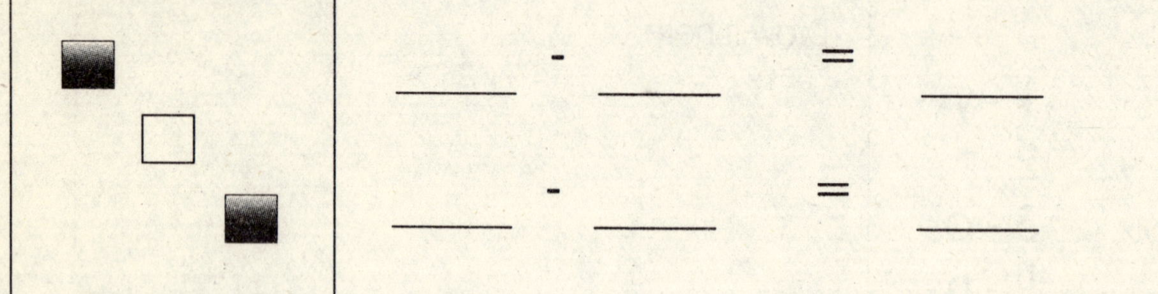

____ - ____ = ____

____ - ____ = ____

____ - ____ = ____

____ - ____ = ____

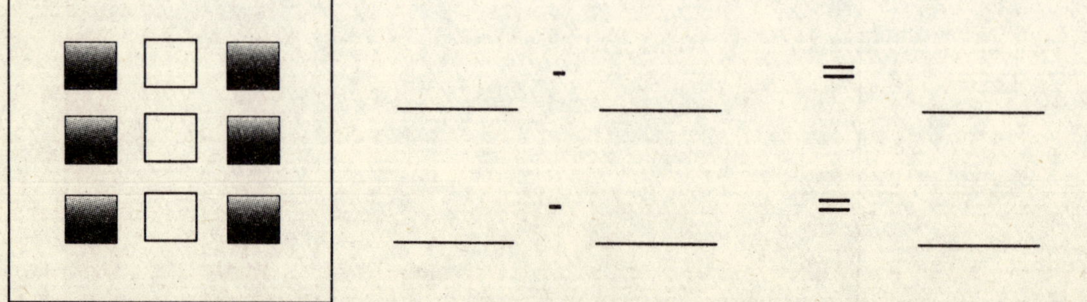

____ - ____ = ____

____ - ____ = ____

Review

8 - 6 = ____

8 - 4 = ____

8 - 7 = ____

8 - 3 = ____

8 - 8 = ____

8 - 1 = ____

8 - 2 = ____

8 - 5 = ____

9 - 4 = ____

9 - 6 = ____

9 - 2 = ____

9 - 7 = ____

9 - 8 = ____

9 - 5 = ____

9 - 3 = ____

9 - 1 = ____

9	8	8	9	9
-3	-6	-2	-5	-8

8	8	9	8	9
-4	-2	-1	-7	-4

Start at 0 to make the tree trunk.

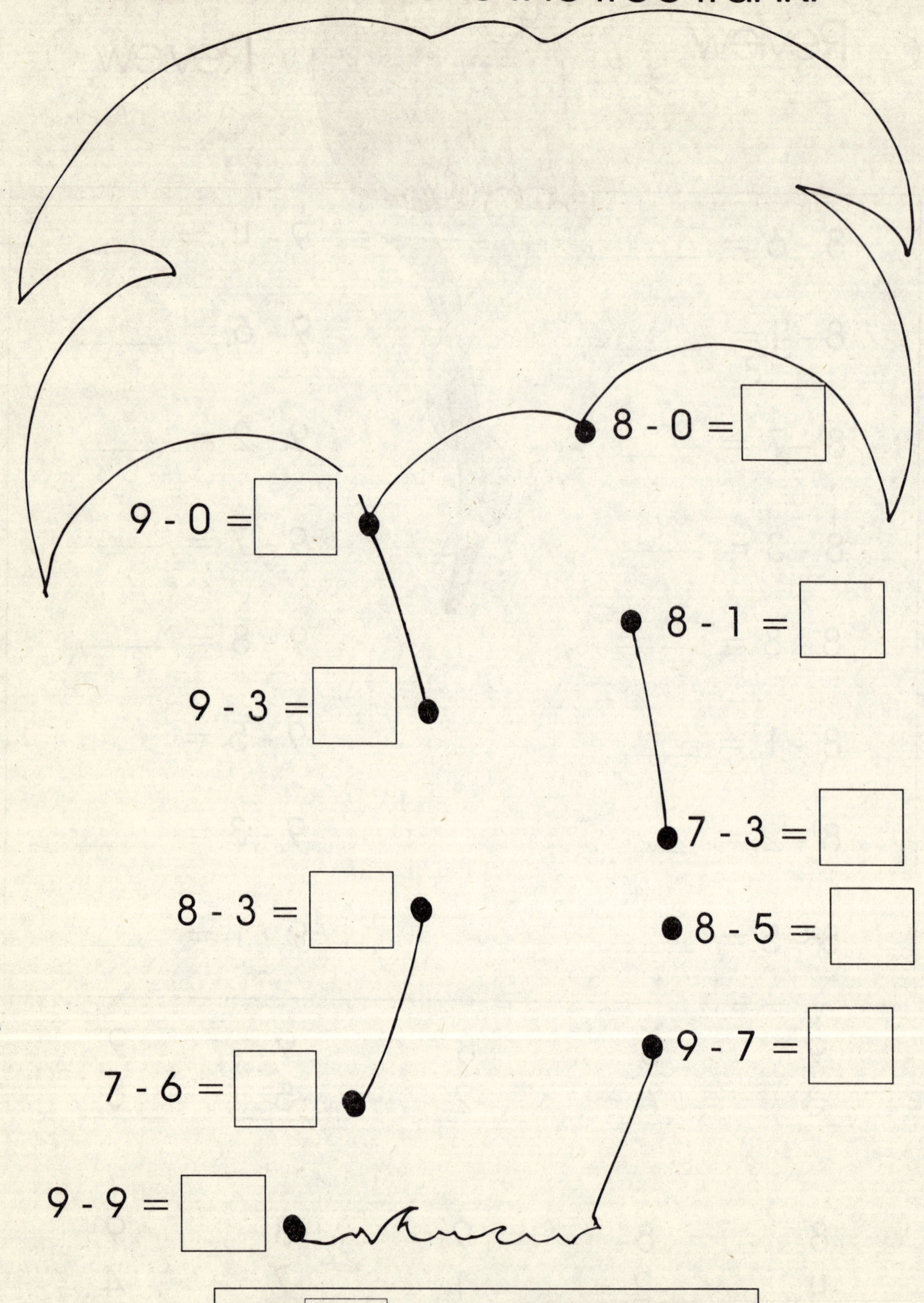

Put 9 - 3 coconuts in the tree.
Put 8 - 7 monkeys in the tree.

What has 4 wheels and flies?

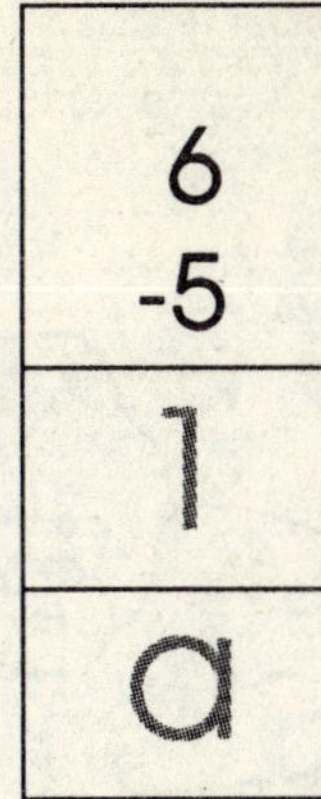

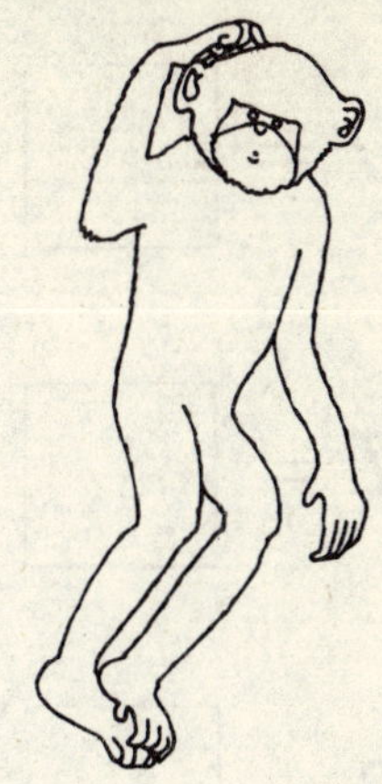

9 -7	8 -7	6 -3	9 -5	3 -2	4 -2	9 -4

7 -1	8 -5	9 -2	9 -1	9 -0

1 - a	4 - b	7 - u
2 - g	5 - e	8 - c
3 - r	6 - t	9 - k

What is the rule?

9 - 9 = ☐

7 - 7 = ☐

3 - 3 = ☐

5 - 5 = ☐

8 - 8 = ☐

1 - 1 = ☐

4 - 4 = ☐

2 - 2 = ☐

6 - 6 = ☐

1 - 0 = ☐

7 - 0 = ☐

2 - 0 = ☐

9 - 0 = ☐

8 - 0 = ☐

6 - 0 = ☐

3 - 0 = ☐

5 - 0 = ☐

4 - 0 = ☐

A number minus itself is always zero.
A number minus zero stays the same.

What is the rule?

9	6	5	2
-1	-1	-1	-1
___	___	___	___

8	4	7	3
-1	-1	-1	-1
___	___	___	___

One less.

8 9	___ 4	___ 1	___ 5
___ 3	___ 8	___ 6	___ 2

Think about the rule.
Tell the rule to someone
in your family.

What's my name?

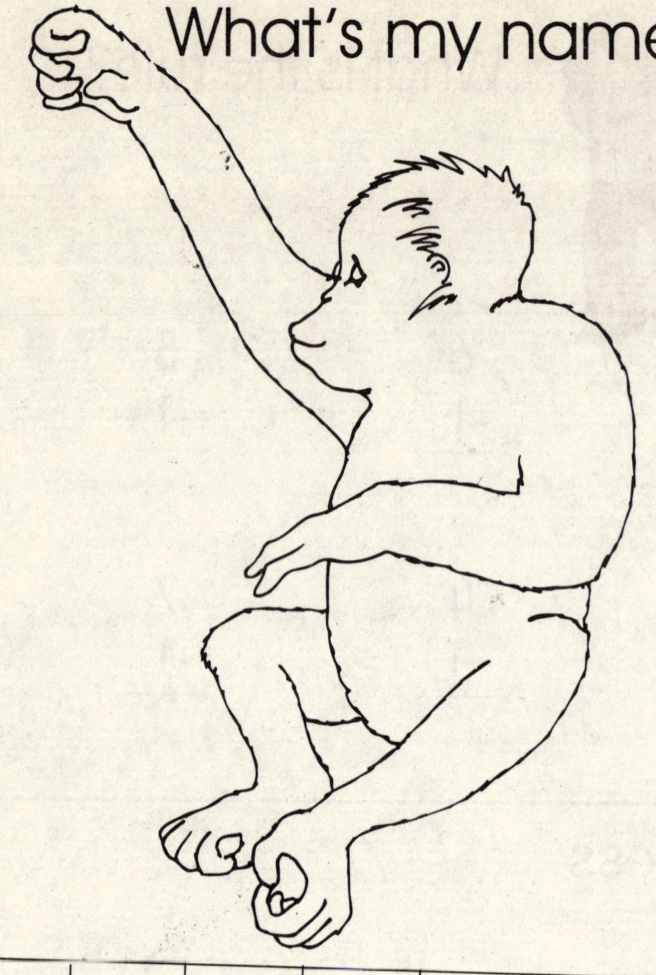

9 -3	7 -0	9 -8	8 -3	9 -6	9 -0	9 -1	8 -7	9 -4
		1						
		a						

1 - a
2 - e
3 - g
4 - m

5 - n
6 - o
7 - r
8 - t

9 - u
10 - k
11 - p
12 - y

Make a match.

9 - 5	2	8 - 0	3
7 - 1	6	6 - 2	4
6 - 4	4	9 - 6	5
5 - 2	3	7 - 2	8

7 - 1	2	9 - 8	1
9 - 7	5	7 - 4	2
8 - 3	3	4 - 2	5
6 - 3	6	6 - 1	3

9 - 4	2	8 - 5	5
7 - 0	5	9 - 1	8
8 - 6	7	7 - 2	0
5 - 2	3	6 - 6	3

What's missing?

3 + 2 = 5

☐ + 4 = 7

4 + ☐ = 10

☐ + 3 = 6

3 + ☐ = 8

☐ + 2 = 4

8 + ☐ = 9

☐ + 5 = 7

1 + ☐ = 5

☐ + 2 = 8

6 + ☐ = 9

☐ + 8 = 12

4 + ☐ = 8

☐ + 5 = 9

4 + ☐ = 6

☐ + 1 = 4

3 + ☐ = 10

☐ + 5 = 6

Subtract to Check Addition

$3 + 4 = 7$	$7 - 3 = 4$	$7 - 4 = 3$
$1 + 3 = 4$	$4 - 1 = 3$	$4 - 3 = 1$
$2 + 7 = $ ___	___	___
$4 + 2 = $ ___	___	___
$7 + 1 = $ ___	___	___
$3 + 5 = $ ___	___	___
$6 + 3 = $ ___	___	___
$2 + 6 = $ ___	___	___

Help the monkey find the bananas.

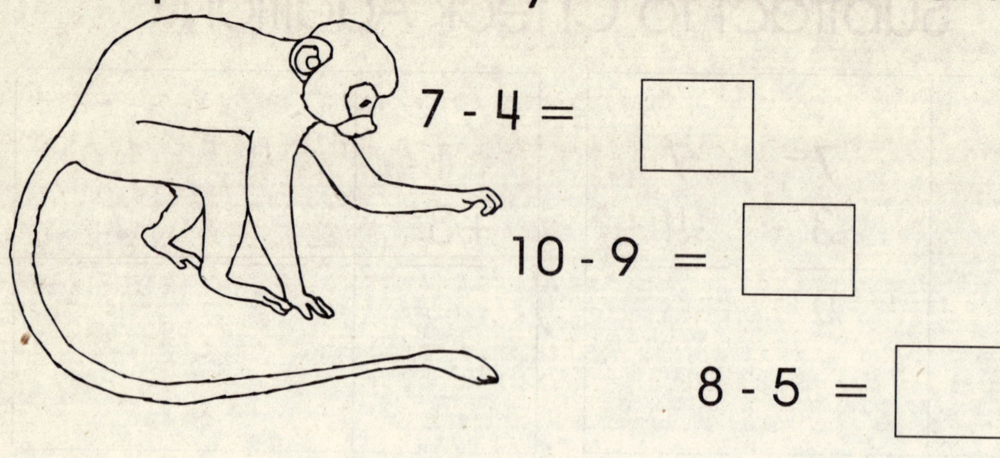

7 - 4 = ☐

10 - 9 = ☐

8 - 5 = ☐

9 - 6 = ☐

6 - 4 = ☐

7 - 7 = ☐

6 - 5 = ☐

9 - 2 = ☐

3 - 3 = ☐

5 - 4 = ☐

1 - 0 = ☐

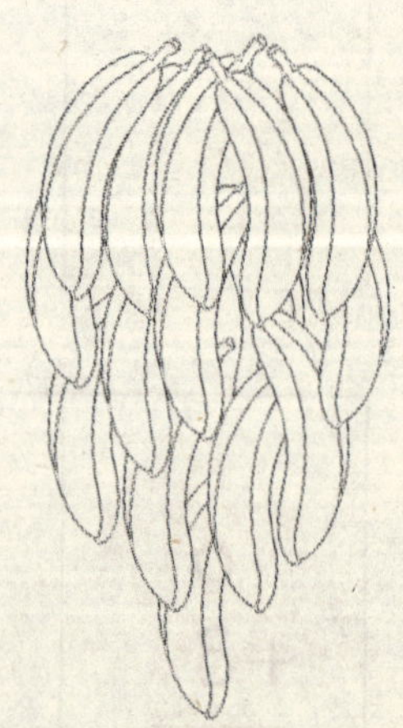

6 - 4 = ☐

Start with 10.

10 - 4 = 6

___ - ___ = ___

___ - ___ = ___

___ - ___ = ___

___ - ___ = ___

___ - ___ = ___

___ - ___ = ___

___ - ___ = ___

___ - ___ = ___

Connect the dots.
Start at 1.

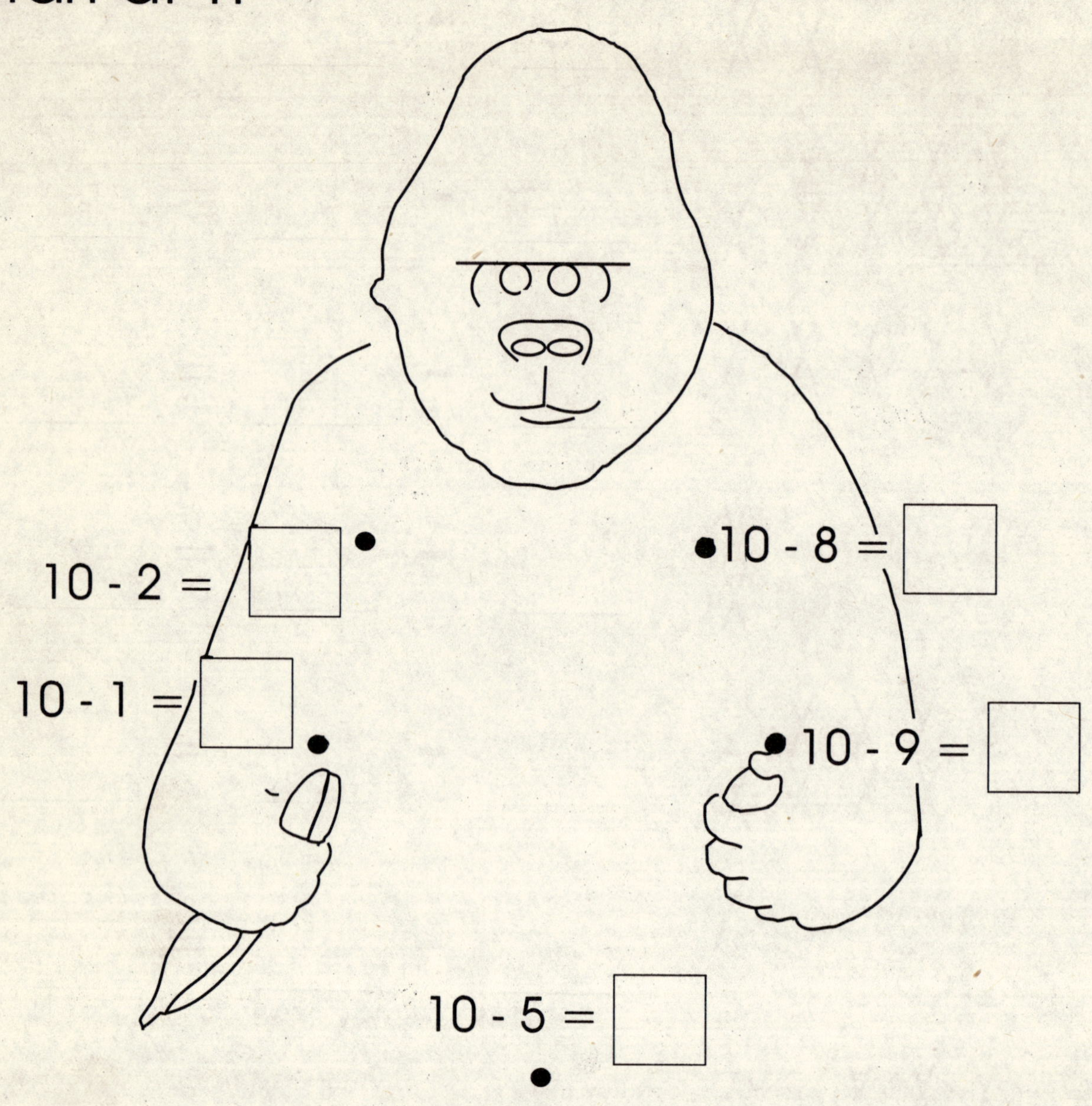

10 - 3 =

10 - 7 =

10 - 4 =

10 - 6 =

Practice Time

8 -5	10 -6	8 -3	9 -5
10 -5	9 -6	10 - 2	8 -4
9 -3	10 -9	8 -6	10 - 7

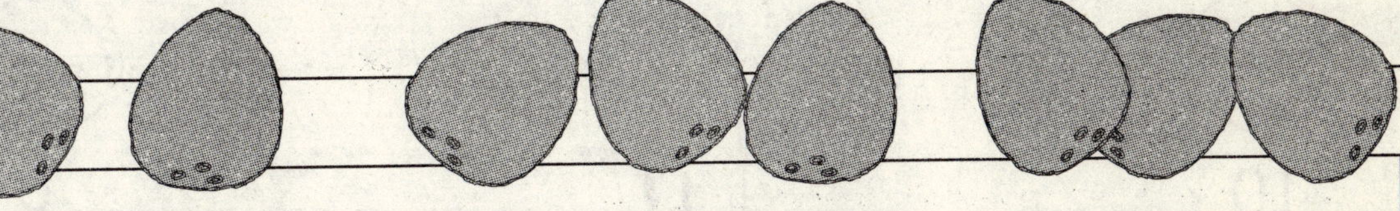

10 - 4 = ______ 8 - 5 = ______

8 - 1 = ______ 10 - 3 = ______

10 - 10 = ______ 8 - 2 = ______

9 - 7 = ______ 10 - 0 = ______

9 - 2 = ______ 10 - 1 = ______

10 - 8 = ______ 9 - 5 = ______

Put the monkeys in their trees.

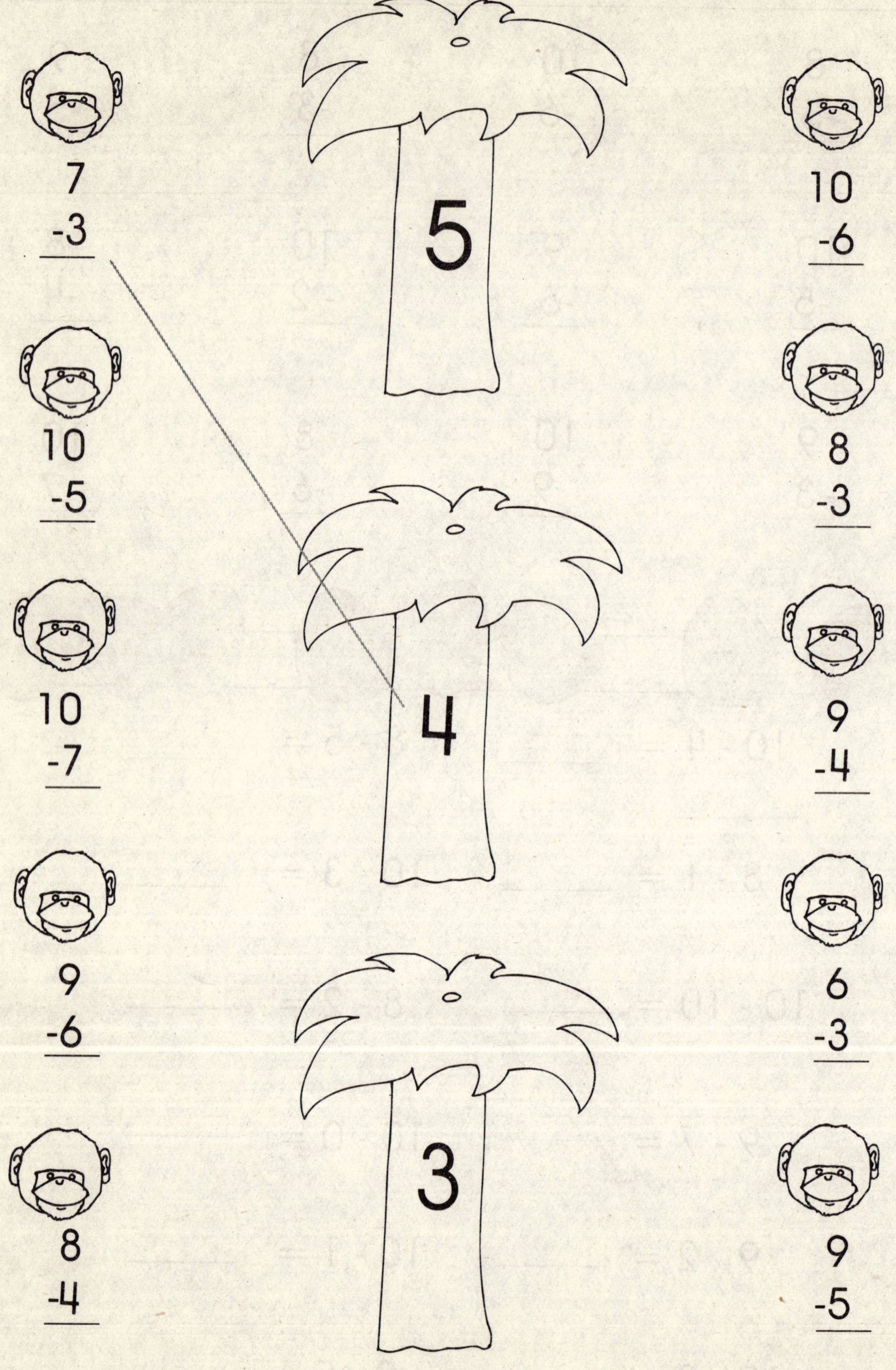

Review

Can you do all of these?

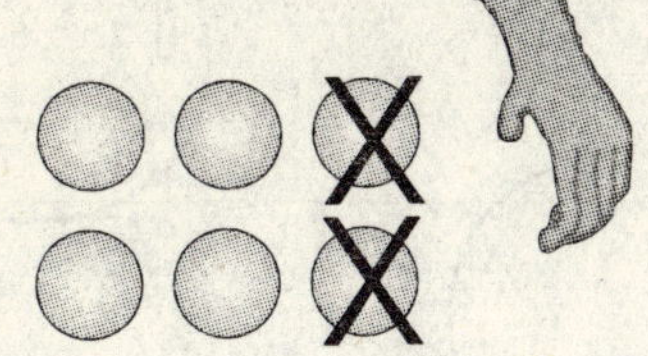

6 - 2 = _____ 4 - 1 = _____

3 - 2 = _____ 4 - 0 = _____

5 - 4 = _____ 3 - 1 = _____

2 - 2 = _____ 5 - 2 = _____

$$\begin{array}{r} 6 \\ -4 \\ \hline \end{array} \quad \begin{array}{r} 5 \\ -3 \\ \hline \end{array} \quad \begin{array}{r} 7 \\ -0 \\ \hline \end{array} \quad \begin{array}{r} 6 \\ -6 \\ \hline \end{array}$$

$$\begin{array}{r} 8 \\ -1 \\ \hline \end{array} \quad \begin{array}{r} 2 \\ -2 \\ \hline \end{array} \quad \begin{array}{r} 4 \\ -4 \\ \hline \end{array} \quad \begin{array}{r} 9 \\ -0 \\ \hline \end{array}$$

Colour 5 blue.
Colour 3 red.
Colour 2 yellow.

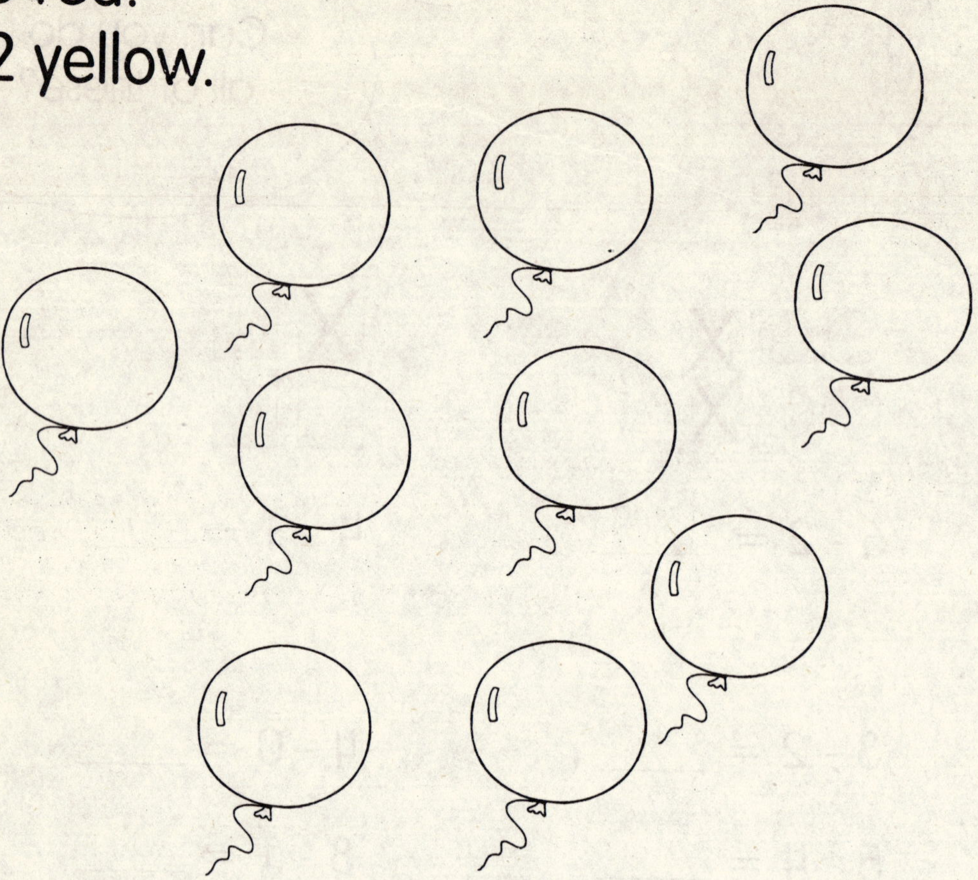

1. How many are there?

blue red yellow

2. How many more blue than yellow?

3. How many more red than yellow?

4. If 3 balloons broke, how many would you have?

Answer Key

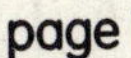

Please take time to go over the work your child has completed. Ask your child to explain what he/she has done. Praise both success and effort. If mistakes have been made, explain what the answer should have been and how to find it. Let your child know that mistakes are a part of learning. The time you spend with your child helps let him/her know you feel learning is important.

page 1

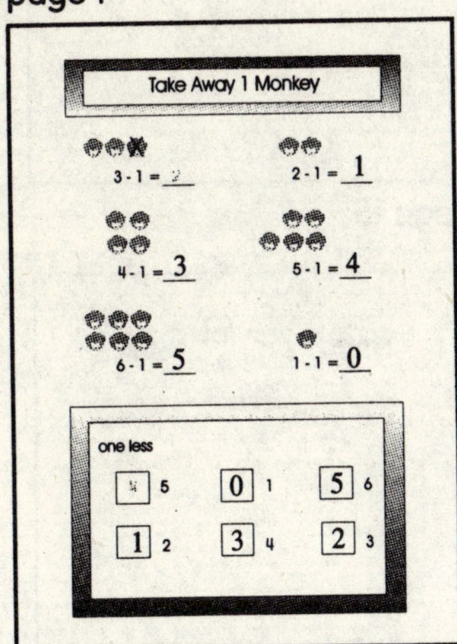

page 2

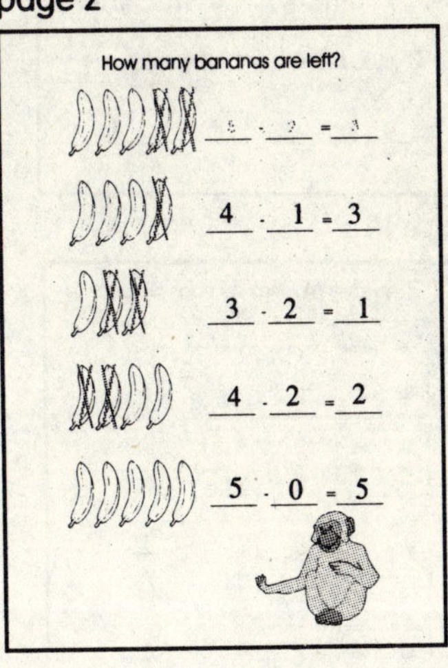

page 3

page 4

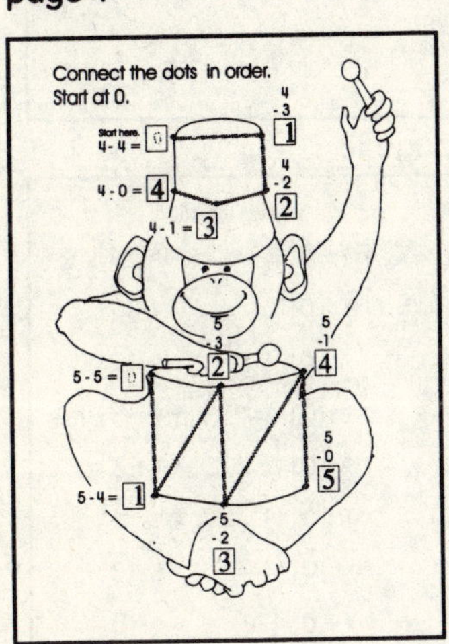

page 5

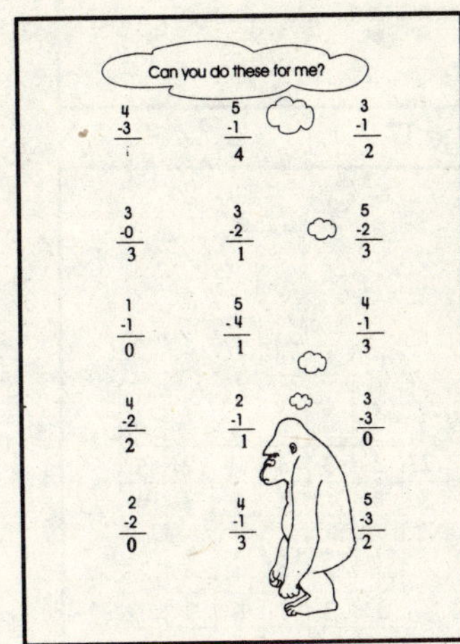

page 6

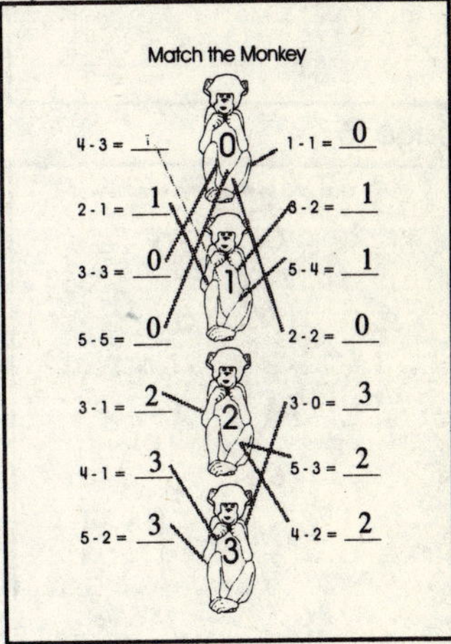

page 7

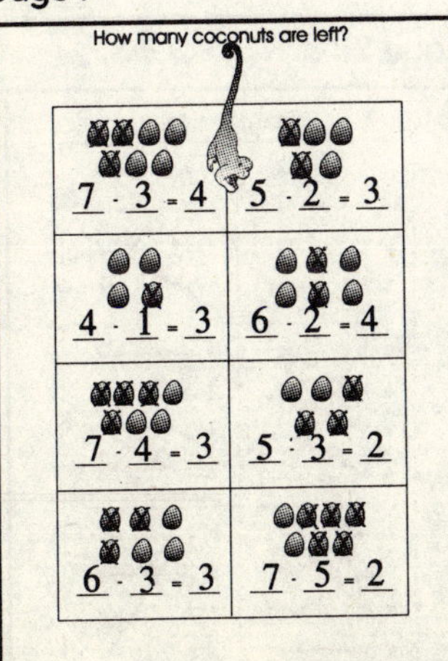

page 8

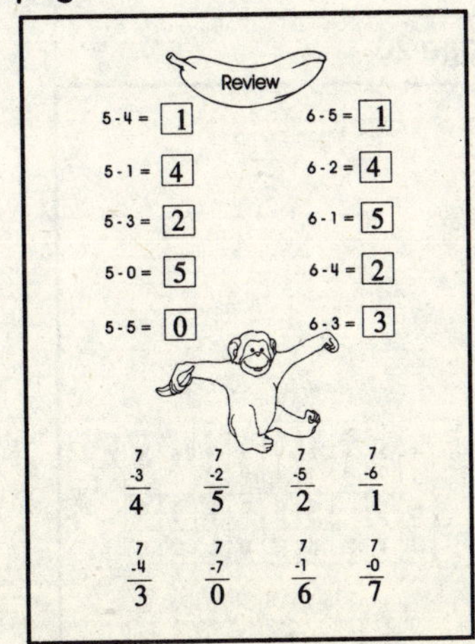

page 9

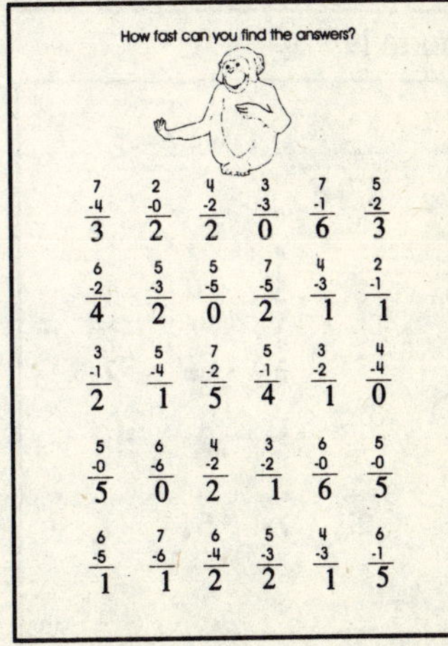

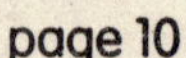

page 10

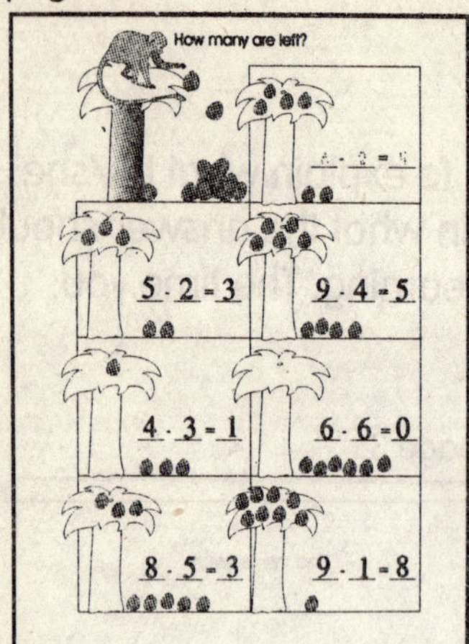

How many are left?

5 - 2 = 3 | 9 - 4 = 5
4 - 3 = 1 | 6 - 6 = 0
8 - 5 = 3 | 9 - 1 = 8

page 11

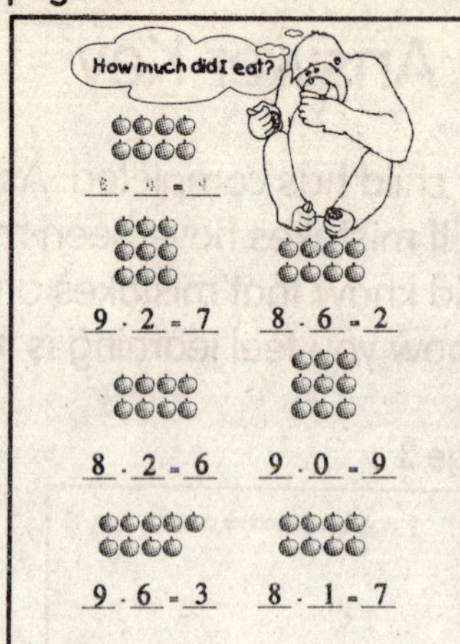

How much did I eat?

9 - 2 = 7 | 8 - 6 = 2
8 - 2 = 6 | 9 - 0 = 9
9 - 6 = 3 | 8 - 1 = 7

page 12

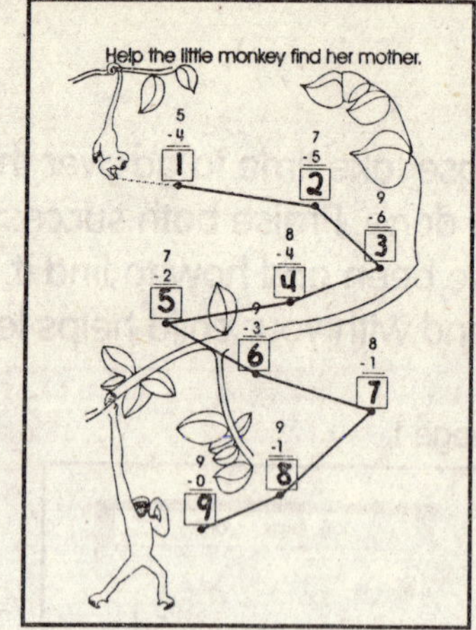

Help the little monkey find her mother.

page 13

You can find this "key" in the jungle.

8 -3	4 -1	6 -2	9 -3	8 -0	7 -6
5	3	4	6	8	1
m	o	n	k	e	y

1 - y, 2 - f, 3 - o, 4 - n, 5 - m, 6 - k, 7 - j, 8 - e, 9 - d, 10 - a

Draw it here.

Pictures will vary but should show a monkey.

page 14

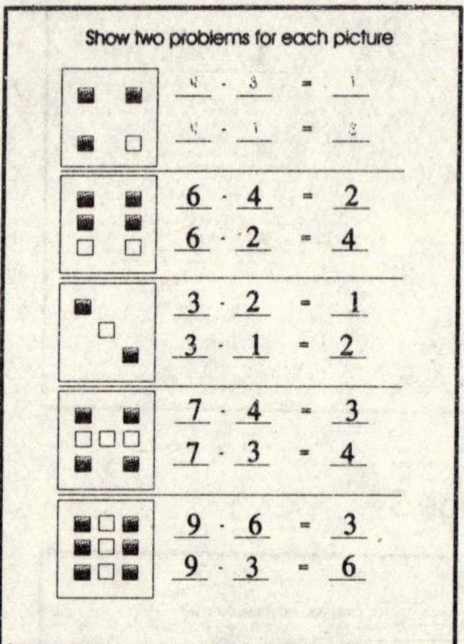

Show two problems for each picture

6 - 4 = 2
6 - 2 = 4
3 - 2 = 1
3 - 1 = 2
7 - 4 = 3
7 - 3 = 4
9 - 6 = 3
9 - 3 = 6

page 15

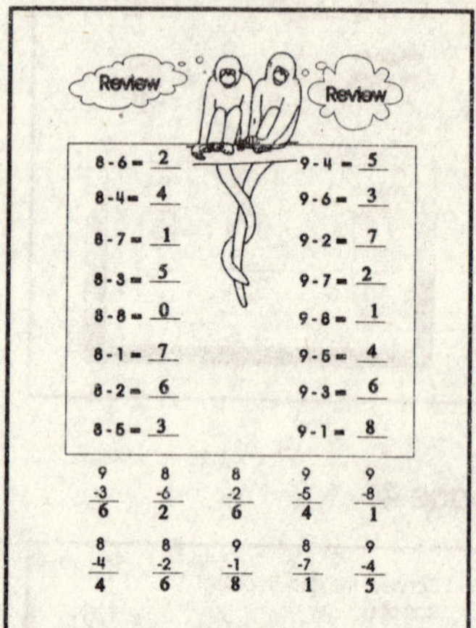

Review

8 - 6 = 2 | 9 - 4 = 5
8 - 4 = 4 | 9 - 6 = 3
8 - 7 = 1 | 9 - 2 = 7
8 - 3 = 5 | 9 - 7 = 2
8 - 8 = 0 | 9 - 8 = 1
8 - 1 = 7 | 9 - 5 = 4
8 - 2 = 6 | 9 - 3 = 6
8 - 5 = 3 | 9 - 1 = 8

page 16

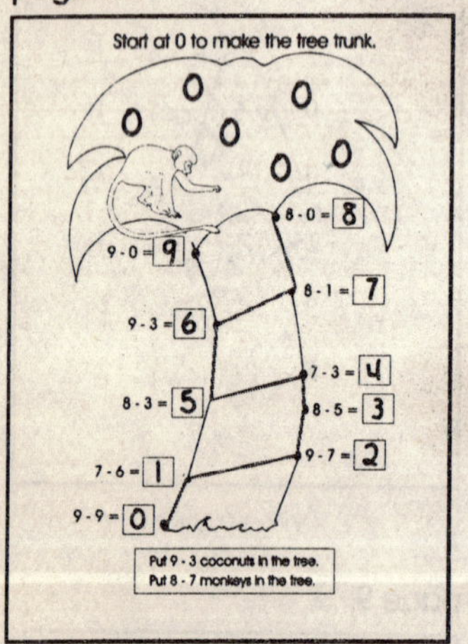

Start at 0 to make the tree trunk.

Put 9 - 3 coconuts in the tree.
Put 8 - 7 monkeys in the tree.

page 17

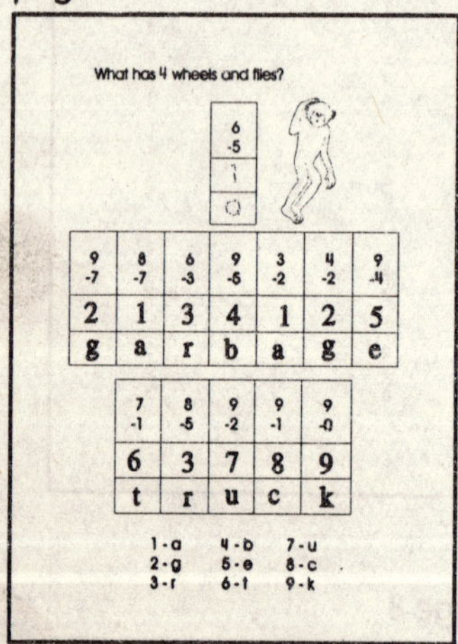

What has 4 wheels and flies?

9 -7	8 -7	6 -3	9 -5	3 -2	4 -2	9 -4
2	1	3	4	1	2	5
g	a	r	b	a	g	e

7 -1	8 -5	9 -2	9 -1	9 -0
6	3	7	8	9
t	r	u	c	k

1 - a, 2 - g, 3 - r, 4 - b, 5 - e, 6 - t, 7 - u, 8 - c, 9 - k

page 18

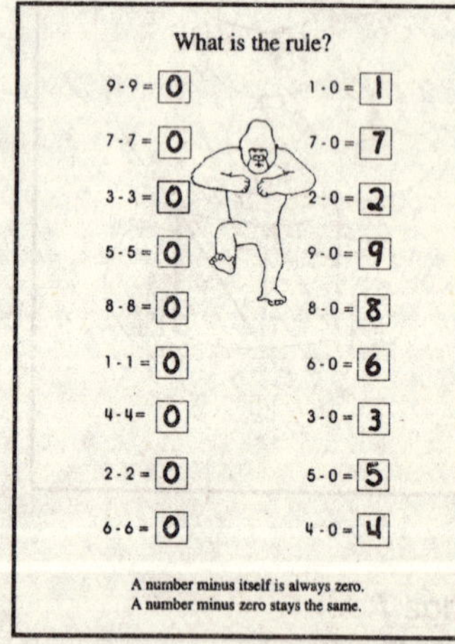

What is the rule?

9 - 9 = 0 | 1 - 0 = 1
7 - 7 = 0 | 7 - 0 = 7
3 - 3 = 0 | 2 - 0 = 2
5 - 5 = 0 | 9 - 0 = 9
8 - 8 = 0 | 8 - 0 = 8
1 - 1 = 0 | 6 - 0 = 6
4 - 4 = 0 | 3 - 0 = 3
2 - 2 = 0 | 5 - 0 = 5
6 - 6 = 0 | 4 - 0 = 4

A number minus itself is always zero.
A number minus zero stays the same.

page 19

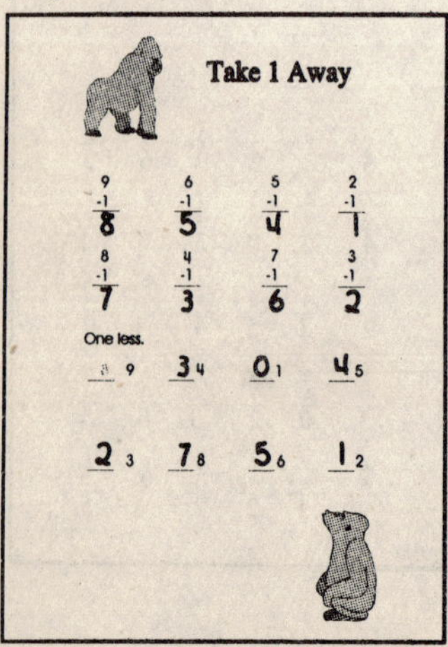

Take 1 Away

One less.

page 20

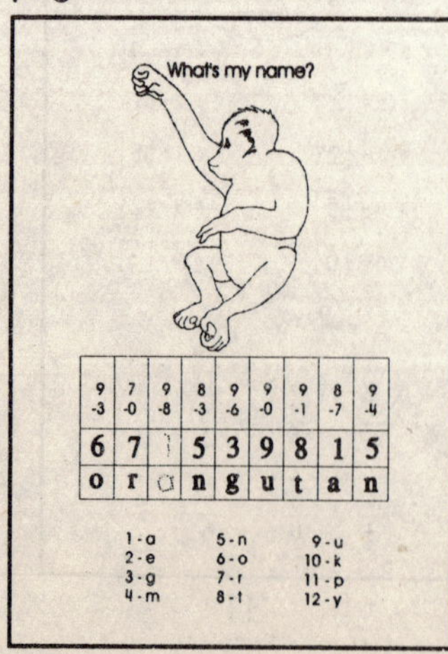

What's my name?

9 -3	7 -0	9 -8	8 -3	9 -6	9 -0	9 -1	8 -7	9 -4
6	7	1	5	3	9	8	1	5
o	r	a	n	g	u	t	a	n

1 - a, 2 - e, 3 - g, 4 - m, 5 - n, 6 - o, 7 - r, 8 - t, 9 - u, 10 - k, 11 - p, 12 - y

page 21

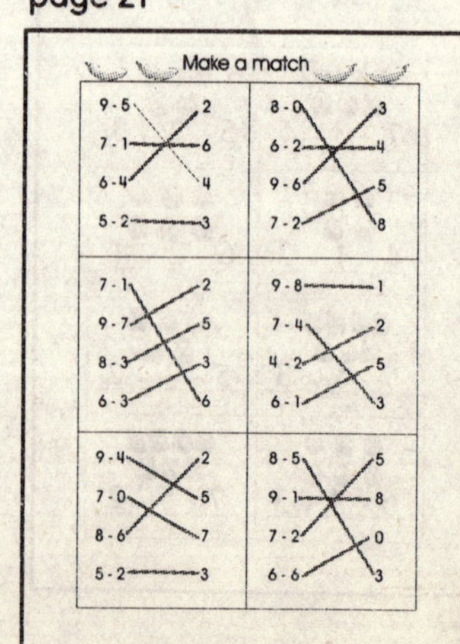

Make a match